The Great Exhibition

Jane Shuter

Heinemann LIBRARY

www.heinemann.co.uk/library
Visit our website to find out more information about **Heinemann Library** books.

To order:
☎ Phone 44 (0) 1865 888066
🗎 Send a fax to 44 (0) 1865 314091
💻 Visit the Heinemann Bookshop at www.heinemann.co.uk/library to browse our catalogue and order online.

First published in Great Britain by Heinemann Library, Halley Court, Jordan Hill, Oxford OX2 8EJ, part of Harcourt Education.
Heinemann is a registered trademark of Harcourt Education Ltd.

Editorial: Lucy Thunder and Helen Cox
Design: David Poole and Geoff Ward
Illustrations: Gerry Ball at Eikon Illustration
Picture Research: Hannah Taylor
Production: Séverine Ribierre

Originated by Repro Multi Warna
Printed and bound in Hong Kong, China by South China Printing

ISBN 0 431 12347 0 (hardback)
07 06 05 04 03
10 9 8 7 6 5 4 3 2 1

ISBN 0 431 12352 7 (paperback)
08 07 06 05 04
10 9 8 7 6 5 4 3 2 1

British Library Cataloguing in Publication Data
Shuter, Jane
How do we know about the Great Exhibition?
907.4'421
A full catalogue record for this book is available from the British Library.

Acknowledgements
The publishers would like to thank the following for permission to reproduce photographs: Antiquarian Images pp**4**, **24**; Bridgeman Art Library p**5**; Hulton Archive p**20**; Illustrated London News p**18**; London Metropolitan Archive p**21**; Mary Evans Picture Library p**19**; Natural History Museum p**27**; Royal Archives p**25**; Victoria & Albert Museum pp**22**, **23**, **26**.

Cover painting of the Great Exhibition in 1851, reproduced with permission of Mary Evans Picture Library.

The publishers would like to thank Rebecca Vickers for her assistance in the preparation of this book.

Every effort has been made to contact copyright holders of any material reproduced in this book. Any omissions will be rectified in subsequent printings if notice is given to the publishers.

Contents

Any words shown in the text in bold, **like this**, are explained in the Glossary.

Heart of an empire

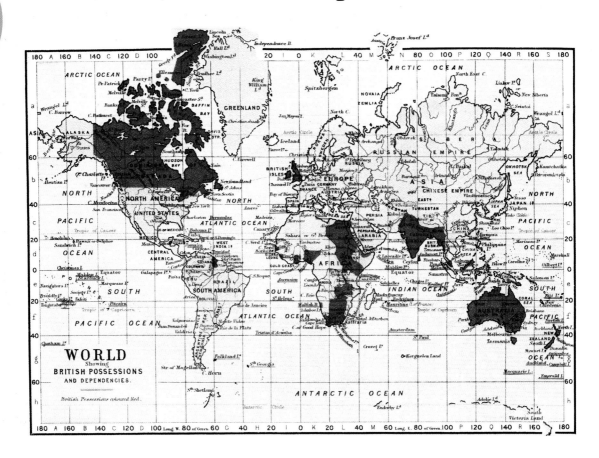

WORLD
Showing
BRITISH POSSESSIONS
AND DEPENDENCIES.

British Possessions coloured Red.

In 1850, Britain was a rich and powerful country ruled by Queen Victoria. It also ran many other countries, which were part of the British **Empire**. These are shown in red on the map.

At that time, British inventors were proud of their machines. **Politicians** suggested holding a Great **Exhibition** to display them and other world inventions.

Help from a prince

Queen Victoria's husband, Prince Albert, was interested in the plan. He got other important people and the rulers of different countries interested, too.

The **committee** organizing the Great **Exhibition** needed a big open space in London to hold the huge event. Prince Albert offered them Hyde Park, which belonged to the Queen.

Choosing a building

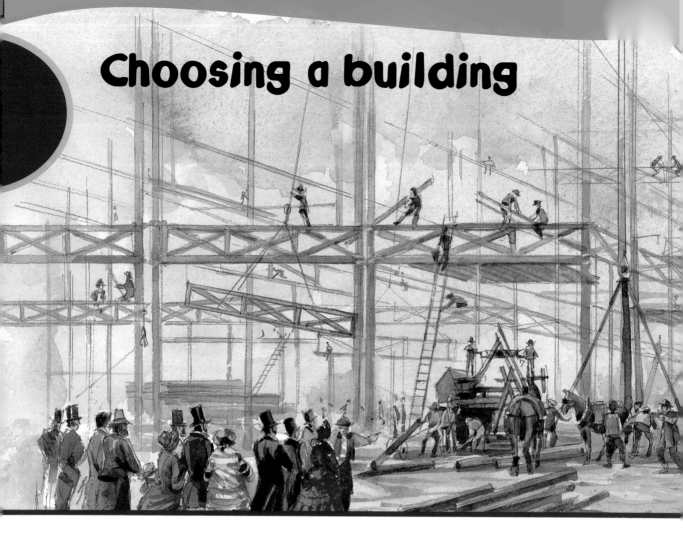

The building for the **Exhibition** could not stay in Hyde Park forever. It had to be quick to put up and take down. It could not damage the park, either.

Joseph Paxton's **design** was chosen. The building used so much glass that it was nicknamed the Crystal Palace. It was built to rise above the trees.

Lots of exhibits

Over 100,000 **exhibits** from 50 countries were brought to London by steam train or steamship. The ship bringing exhibits from Russia got stuck in icy seas.

There were many exhibits, from huge steam-run machines to tiny glass buttons. Some exhibits were clever but useless, like a vase made from **lard**.

A grand opening

On 1 May 1851, Queen Victoria opened the Great **Exhibition**. Tickets for that first day cost about £3 and could be reused. The Queen visited it many times.

People came to the Great Exhibition from all over the world. The entry cost ranged from £1 to 1 **shilling** on different days.

Visiting the Great Exhibition

Rich people went to the **Exhibition** when tickets were £1. They travelled in their own **carriages**. Some days only sick people could visit, when the exhibition was less crowded.

Most people went on days when tickets were 1 **shilling**. **Travel agent** Thomas Cook organized cheap trains to London so that more people could see it.

Closing down

On 15 October 1851, the Great **Exhibition** closed. The building was moved to Sydenham, London. It burned down in November 1936.

The Great Exhibition was a big success. It made £186,000 **profit**. Ordinary workers only earned about £50 a year. The money paid for **museums** in London.

How do we know?

People all over the world were interested in the Great **Exhibition**. People drew pictures of the building and wrote and talked about how quickly it was put up.

Many artists painted pictures of the finished building. Some were in colour, like this one. No photos of the Crystal Palace in Hyde Park have survived.

Paintings and photos

Artists painted many pictures of the inside of the Crystal Palace, showing the **exhibition** halls. This painting shows **exhibits** from Turkey.

When the Crystal Palace was moved
to Sydenham, it was made bigger.
A photographer took photos of the
building going back up.

Cartoons

Manchester, in 1851.

The Great **Exhibition** was always in
the news at that time. The newspapers
printed **cartoons** showing what
people thought. These cartoons are
by George Cruikshank.

London, in 1851.

Cruikshank's cartoons show Manchester and London in 1851. They show that the Great Exhibition was so important that everyone wanted to go to it!

Writings

CHAPTER XIV.

PRECIOUS STONES.—MR. HOPE'S COLLECTION—THE DIAMOND, SAPPHIRE, EMERALD, GARNET, ETC.
—QUEEN OF SPAIN'S JEWELS—THE JEWELLED HAWK—PEARLS.

THE high estimation that in all ages has been bestowed upon jewels and precious stones, is perhaps sufficiently to be accounted for, when we take into consideration their essential qualities of light, and colour, and durability; and the correspondence which, in consequence of these valuable attributes, they possess with respect to the more elevated principles in the world of mind. Frequent mention is made of them in Holy Writ, from the breast-plate of Aaron described by Moses, to the sublime account in the Apocalypse of the wonders of the Holy City, its shining courts, and its gates of pearl, in all which description there is doubtless involved some mystic meaning connected with the future glorious destiny of the church, not obviously apparent to the merely superficial or general reader. In the world of poetry, too, constant recurrence is made to the different qualities of precious stones, and their reference to various physical endowments. Mental acuteness, and brilliancy of imagination, are invariably likened to the radiance of the diamond, whilst constancy and truth are equally represented in its unchangeableness and its durability. What can be more appropriate or beautiful than the lines of Collins, where, in illustration of the playfulness of wit and repartee, in one of the characters in his Ode to Music, he says—

"The jewels in whose crisped hair
Were placed each other's beams to share."

And with respect to personal beauty, who among all the votaries of Apollo ever neglected, in speaking of the brilliancy of his mistress's eyes, to compare them to the lustre of the diamond, her teeth to orient pearl, or her lips or her cheeks to the glowing ruby? The treasures of the secret mine have indeed been an inexhaustible source of comparison and metaphor, from the days of old Anacreon to those of his great rival and imitator, of Hibernian celebrity. Pliny, and other early writers on the subject of gems, attributed various occult qualities and miraculous powers to precious stones in general; they were also supposed to possess rare medicinal qualities, an opinion sanctioned by our own great philosopher Boyle, in whose time were to be found in the Materia Medica such compositions as the *Electuarium e Gemmis, Confectio de Hyacinthis*, &c., with which the more opulent of our forefathers endeavoured to ward off the stroke of death. The diamond more particularly enjoyed a high repute for these and other hidden virtues; it was considered as an infallible specific in many diseases, and a test of conjugal fidelity, a reconciler of domestic strife, and an amulet of highest power against poisons, insanity, witchcraft, incantations, nocturnal goblins, and evil spirits.

Never before in the history of the world was there so large a collection of valuable gems and exquisite specimens of the lapidary's art collected in one building as was exhibited in the Crystal Palace. The Exhibition contained the finest diamond, the finest ruby, and the finest emerald known to the world. For a sight of a single one of these stones an adventurous voyager traversed enormous distances two centuries ago, and by dint of extraordinary influence, audacity, and fortune, was enabled to record himself as the only European who had ever succeeded in the attempt. That stone was lately placed in Hyde Park, and might have been seen by any working man in the country for a shilling. The richest collection of treasures ever known was formerly to be found at Dresden. Its existence was due to a singular succession of wealthy and acquisitive

THE EMPEROR OF RUSSIA'S JEWEL CASKET.

HER MAJESTY'S JEWEL CASE.

This **catalogue** of the Great **Exhibition** lists and shows pictures of the **exhibits**. Copies of the catalogue were sold after the Exhibition. Queen Victoria had one.

Letters and diaries from the time describe what people felt about the Great Exhibition. This letter, written by Queen Victoria, describes the Exhibition as 'beautiful' and 'fairy-like'.

Museums

Some **museums** have displays of **souvenirs** from the Great **Exhibition**. Some people bought souvenirs, like this china pot and these special books. Others kept their ticket instead.

The Natural History Museum in London is one of the museums built with money from the Great Exhibition. In this way, the Great Exhibition is still helping people learn today.

Timeline

January 1850 A **committee** is set up to organize a Great **Exhibition**. Prince Albert is one of the people on the committee.

26 July 1850 Joseph Paxton's **design** for the building is chosen.

26 September 1850 First iron column of the building is put up.

April 1851 The first **exhibits** are set up.

1 May 1851 Queen Victoria opens the Great Exhibition.

15 October 1851 The Great Exhibition closes.

1852–4 The Crystal Palace is taken down, made larger and rebuilt in Sydenham, south London.

November 1936 The Crystal Palace burns down during a firework display.

Great Exhibition facts

- It took over 2000 workers just 15 months to build the Crystal Palace.
- There were 6,201,856 visitors to the Great Exhibition.
- They saw over 100,000 exhibits.
- The Great Exhibition made a **profit** of £186,000.

Biographies

Prince Albert

Prince Albert was born in Germany in 1819. He married Queen Victoria in 1840 and lived in England for the rest of his life. Albert was very interested in helping people learn. He made sure that much of the profit from the Great Exhibition was spent on building **museums**. Albert died in 1861.

Thomas Cook

Thomas Cook was born in 1808. He was the first **travel agent**. He ran his first trip in 1841. Passengers went 16 kilometres from Leicester to Loughborough by train. The trip cost 1 **shilling** and included a day out in a park at a fair. Thomas went on to organize trips to the Great Exhibition and tours abroad for rich travellers. He died in 1892.

Joseph Paxton

Joseph Paxton was born in 1801. He trained as an **architect**. In 1826, he went to work for the Duke of Devonshire. Joseph designed his gardens and the buildings in them, including a huge greenhouse. It was this that gave him the idea for his winning design for the Crystal Palace. He died in 1865.

Glossary

architect person who designs buildings

carriage vehicle, pulled by horses, that about four people could travel in

cartoon drawing with either words underneath or speech bubbles for the people in the picture. Cartoons are supposed to be funny and often show what people really think about something.

catalogue list of everything on show in an exhibition, or everything that a shop has to sell. Catalogues usually have pictures.

committee group of people who work together to organize an event or run a business

design drawing to show how something will look when it is made or built

empire a country and all the lands that it controls in other parts of the world

exhibit something that is displayed at an exhibition

exhibition special event, where things are displayed together for people to come and look at

lard pig fat

museum building that has things in it that tell us about the past

politician person who works, or wants to work, in the government

profit amount of money made from something

shilling silver coin used in Victorian times. An ordinary worker earned about 12 shillings a week.

souvenir something bought on a visit to help the person remember a place or event

travel agent person who organizes trips or holidays for other people

Further reading

Life and World of Queen Victoria,
Brian Williams, Heinemann Library, 2001

Index